MY BROTHER'S KEEPER

by
Mary Bertha Attole

1stBooks – rev. 07/24/01

I firmly believe that racism is ethically and morally wrong, and if you believe as I do, then you too must do something, and do it now, so as to insure a better and more peaceful world for all races.

Mary Bertha Attole

To my family and my Catholic faith.

1

Sunlight filters under the half drawn shade of a small window into the front office of the Clarion Police Department. Beneath the window are four chairs.

A simple desk and chair adorns the center of the room. A nameplate on the desk says simply FRONT DESK. The desk is a cluttered mess of papers with a phone peeping out from underneath. A small desk lamp and a red canister filled with assorted pens and pencils are nearby.

Old Glory stands at the far left corner of the room. The room is relatively quiet except for the swishing of the ceiling fan up above and the ticking of the clock on the wall behind the desk.

Behind the desk are two offices. The office where the door has just swung open belongs to the captain. Officer Jeff Franklin, whose boyish charm belies a roguish personality, comes out of the captain's office and shuts the door behind him. He heads toward the front desk, sits down and begins straightening out the papers.

Sitting at the desk in the office with the door partially open is Harley Jefferson, an honest, black detective with a keen eye. On the wall behind him is a portrait of Martin Luther King.

The left handed detective is jotting down notes on a sheet of paper when his attention is diverted to two strange men entering the station. Both are wearing blue jeans and blue jean jackets. On the left sleeve of their jackets is an emblem of the Confederate flag. The ruggedly handsome gentleman goes by the name of Harold Jessup and the burly, wavy haired redneck next to him is Jake Spooner.

Both men approach the front desk. Franklin greets them. "Good morning, gentlemen. What can I do for you?"

Only Jessup speaks. "We'd like to speak to the man in charge."

"That would be Capt. Rafferty. I'll ring him for you."

He rings the office.

"Yes," replies the gravelled voice.

"Captain, there are two gentlemen to see you."

"Okay, I'll be right there."

Franklin hangs up. "He'll be right with you."

Suddenly the captain's door opens and out comes Bill Rafferty, a bitter, thirty year veteran of the Clarion police department and a man consumed by greed. He is carrying three or four manila folders which he hands to Franklin. "Franklin, please file these for me."

"Yes, captain." Franklin gets up. His blue uniform is pressed to a perfect crease.

Rafferty sits in Franklin's chair. "Gentlemen, what can I do for you?"

"My name is Harold Jessup and this is Jake Spooner. We'd like to apply for a permit."

Rafferty takes a form out of the desk drawer and a pencil out of the canister. "Now just what is this permit for?"

"Our organization is sponsoring a march through downtown Clarion on Saturday."

Rafferty proceeds to write on the form. "What's the name of your organization?"

2

"United Klans of America."

Harley, who is still sitting in his office, looks up from his desk and for a moment his eyes meet Jessup's.

"You mean this is a klan march?" asks Rafferty in a slightly pitched voice.

"Yes, sir."

"How many will be marching?"

"There'll be fifty. The others will arrive Saturday."

"I hope this will be a peaceful march."

"It will be."

"It better be." Both men eye each other silently. Then Rafferty breaks the spell. "Why Clarion?"

"Well, I kinda like Clarion. It's a quiet town."

"See that it stays that way."

"Is that a warning, captain?"

"It is and you had better heed it, because if you or your group cause any trouble, I'll throw you in jail so fast, your head will spin. You got that, Mr. Jessup?"

Jessup mimics a salute. "Loud and clear." Spooner grins.

"That'll be twenty five dollars."

Jessup takes out his wallet, takes out a couple of bills and hands them to Rafferty. "See you around, captain."

"I hope not, Mr. Jessup."

Rafferty calls a department meeting to discuss the upcoming Klan march. All members of his department gather around him including

Harley and Franklin. "I called this meeting for a very special purpose. There's going to be a march here on Saturday."

"What kind of march, captain?" asks Franklin.

"It's a klan march, Franklin." There are whispers among the group. "These fellas came in a little while ago for a permit."

"Why did you give them the permit?" asks another officer.

"He had to, Smith," answers Harley. "If he refused, they could sue us for violating their civil rights."

"That may sound awfully weird, but I'm afraid Harley's right. Now I want to make sure there's no trouble in Clarion. I'm going to put extra patrols on the streets and I want everyone's cooperation. Is that clear?"

"Yes, sir."

"I think that's about it. Any questions?"

"No, sir."

"Well, since there aren't any questions, you all can get back to work. Thank you."

2

The Jefferson family is seated at the dining room table celebrating daughter Stacy's sixteenth birthday. They are surrounded by happy faced teenagers. The room is brightly lit. Decorations abound. On the table are all the essentials of a birthday party, including a beautifully decorated cake with sixteen candles and the words Happy Birthday.

Harley is seated at the far left. Roz, his former high school sweetheart and wife of eighteen years, is on his left. Jamie, their adorable, wide eyed, four year old son, is seated across from them on a high chair. Stacy, a sweet, cheerful teenager with smiling eyes, is at the head of the table in the seat of honor. She is about to blow out the candles on her cake while everyone sings Happy Birthday. "Happy birthday to you, happy birthday to you, happy birthday, dear Stacy. Happy birthday to you."

She blows out all the candles. Everyone applauds. "Thanks everyone. This is the nicest birthday I've ever had."

"Well, I'm glad you're enjoying yourself," says Harley.

"Oh, daddy, I am. Just being here with my family and friends is the nicest present I could ever have."

"That's so sweet, Stacy," says Roz.

Doorbell rings. "I'll get it," volunteers Harley. He gets up and goes toward the door. Portraits of Jefferson family members, past and present, line the hallway leading to the door. Harley opens the door. Standing there is Steve Marks, the black, hot shot investigative reporter for the

5

<u>Clarion</u> <u>Gazette</u>, Harley's best friend and Stacy's godfather. "Steve, you're right on time."

"You know I wouldn't miss Stacy's sixteenth birthday."

"Come in."

"Thanks."

"Come on. Everyone's in the dining room."

They make their way to the dining room. When Stacy sees Steve, she runs to hug him. "Hi, Steve."

"Happy birthday, Stacy." He hands her a present.

"Thanks. Come in and have a piece of cake."

"Okay, one piece, but I can't stay long. Hi, Roz." He kisses her.

"Hi, Steve. Glad you could make it."

"I wouldn't have missed it for the world. After all she is my favorite goddaughter."

Stacy hands him a piece of cake. "But Steve, I'm your only goddaughter." Everyone laughs.

Steve sits next to Jamie and proceeds to tickle him. "Hey, little buddy." The child, whose mouth is pasted with cake, giggles. Steve takes a bite of his cake. "Good cake."

"Yeah," answers Stacy. "Mom made it." Roz smiles.

"Are you working tonight, Steve?" asks Harley.

"Yeah, I'm meeting a contact." He looks at his watch. "Oh, look at the time. Sorry, folks, but I've got to go."

"But you haven't finished your cake," says Stacy.

"I'll take it with me." He gets up from the table and grabs his paper plate. "Bye, Stacy" He kisses her on the forehead. "Thanks for the cake."

"Bye, Steve. Thanks for the present."

"Sure. Bye, Roz and Jamie."

"Take care."

Harley walks Steve to the door. "You be careful."

"I will."

3

Steve Marks enters the Magnolia Lounge. The place is dimly lit. On the wall, above the bar, is a neon sign of a magnolia and the word magnolia written beneath it in longhand. It is happy hour and the lounge is full of patrons. Some are sitting at the bar, while others are sitting at the tables. On the bar and on the tables are small, foil like trays with red Magnolia Lounge matchhooks. The words Magnolia Lounge are written in longhand on each matchbook with bold, black lettering. Steve goes to a table to meet his contact. Weasel is a shady character with whiskers on his pointed face, long, stringy hair and drooping eyes.

"Hey, man."

"Hey, Steve."

"So what have you got for me, Weasel?"

"It's big, man. Real big."

"What' s big?"

"Word on the street is there's a drug deal going down in the park tonight."

"What's so important about a drug deal?"

"Not what, but who."

"What do you mean? Who?"

"Cops. That's who."

"What! Are you saying cops are involved?"

"Yes."

"Are you sure?"

"Yes. I got it from a reliable source."

"Did your source say whether they were selling or buying drugs?"

"Selling."

"I wonder where they're getting the drugs."

"Beats me."

"This could be big news."

"Yeah, man, but you'd better be careful."

"I will. Thanks." He hands Weasel a twenty dollar bill.

"Okay, man. Check you later."

Steve gets up. As he makes his way through the crowd, he accidentally bumps into Jessup, who has just entered the lounge, accompanied by Spooner. "Excuse me."

"Hey, boy, you'd better watch where you're going."

"I said I was sorry."

Both men casts sarcastic glances at Steve. "I didn't hear you. Did you, Jake?"

"No. I didn't hear a thing."

Steve points his right index finger at them. "Look! I don't want any trouble. If you didn't hear me the first time, well, that's just too bad."

Spooner begins to provoke Steve. "Where are your manners, boy? Don't you know it's impolite to point?"

His blood boiling, Steve's voice rises. "Don't call me boy."

The provocation continues. "You know there was a time when a nigger like you would he hung for pointing at a white man."

Steve grabs Spooner by the collar. "You son of a bitch."

9

Jessup grabs Steve and tries to pull him off of Spooner. They are interrupted by the bartender, a no nonsense, middle aged man with a gruff appearance. "Hey, what's the trouble?."

"No trouble," responds Spooner.

"It didn't seem that way to me. Steve, are you okay?"

"Yeah. We just had a little misunderstanding."

The bartender looks at Steve and then at Jessup and Spooner. "Look! I saw what happened. Now I don't want any trouble. It's bad for business. So why don' t you two go on about your business."

"Come on, Jake. Let's go find a table."

"Sure."

They disappear into the crowd, while Steve and the bartender remain standing. "Thanks, man. I owe you one."

"Don't mention it, Steve. I was glad to help. After all they're not exactly my kind of folks."

"Mine either. Take care."

"You too."

Steve leaves and the bartender goes back to the bar. Meanwhile Jessup and Spooner are seated at a table when a perky, young woman in a skin tight, low cut dress, approaches them. "Which one of you fellas will buy me a beer?"

Spooner casts a lustful glance at her. "I will, honey. Just sit right down here." She sits next to him. He yells to a passing waiter. "A beer for the lady."

"Coming right up."

"Hi. I'm Cindy James."

"Hi, Cindy. I'm Jake Spooner and this is Harold Jessup."

"Hi."

The waiter brings her beer. "Thank you." Waiter leaves. She takes a sip of beer. "You fellas want to have some fun tonight?"

"Sure, honey. What have you got in mind?"

"Why don't you two come back to my place and find out? Harold, I'll even introduce you to one of my girlfriends."

"We'd like that, wouldn't we, Harold?"

"No, not tonight, but you go ahead, Jake. I'm going to go for a walk, then head back to the motel."

"Okay."

"Are you ready, Jake?" asks Cindy.

"Sure."

"Wait. I'll walk out with you two," adds Jessup. As he gets up from the table, he grabs one of the matchbooks from the tray. As they leave, the bartender watches them.

The brass lamp is the only light illuminating through Cindy's simple bedroom. Cindy and Jake are standing near the small bed embracing. Their bodies cling to each other like magnets. After embracing, they ogle each other, while mentally undressing each other.

"Kiss me, Jake."

"Oh, yes."

Then Spooner's lips crushingly descend upon Cindy's luscious, ruby lips, enveloping her voluptuous mouth. The strangers grope each other's willing bodies in the dark of night, uncertain of what hidden desires lie in

11

the recesses of their imaginations. Spooner's strong, masculine hands glide down her back sending endless shivers through every fiber of her being. She moans. Finally his hands come to rest upon her firm, round, sensuous buttocks, softly caressing them, which titilates him immeasurably. He groans.

Traces of sweat lingers on their foreheads. After what seems like an eternity, their lips part. They gasp simultaneously.

"More?" asks Spooner.

"Yes, please."

Eyes closed, Cindy tilts her head backward, while Spooner buries his hungry mouth on the side of her small, ivory neck, like Dracula descending upon an unsuspecting victim. His mouth travels up and down her neck. Then slowly it finds its way back to her eagerly awaiting lips. She moans.

Meanwhile, Cindy's soft hands caress the back of Spooner's neck and strokes his wavy hair. She brings her trembling hands down his chest and hurriedly fumbles with the buttons on his shirt, managing to unbutton them all. She pulls it from the waistband of his jeans, off his broad shoulders and from his arms onto the floor. Her hands move up and down his strong back, then around to the front to massage his hairy chest, while he lets out a deep, throaty moan. For a moment, her sensuous mouth leaves his to plant tiny, wet kisses on his chest.

"Oh, God."

Slowly his wandering hands find her zipper. With his right hand, he slowly unzips her dress and with both hands, pulls it off her shoulders. She lifts her arms out of the dress and lets it fall on the floor. Spooner's eyes are glued to the sexy, black and red, silk, lace teddy hugging her smooth, ivory skin. Her gorgeous breasts bulge through the thin lining of her teddy. He can even see the lining of her nipples. His hands go up and down her beautiful thighs, then around to the front to feel her firm breasts. He then buries his face in her bosom. Finally he squeezes her beautifully curved body to his. His ravenous mouth kisses her eagerly awaiting lips with a burning passion which almost takes their breaths away and sends them into complete arousal.

"I want you," gasps Spooner.

"Take me."

Spooner pulls the teddy off of Cindy's shoulders, while she turns out the lamp.

4

As Steve is walking through the park, the sounds of chirping crickets filters through the crisp night air. Around his neck hangs his prized Minolta camera. Suddenly he hears voices. He stops and peeps through the bushes. He notices three men standing not too far away. They seem deep in conversation. Steve recognizes all three. Tyrone Hudson, a Jamaican with shoulder length braids, is a local, two bit drug dealer who has set up shop in Clarion. He is holding a briefcase. The other two are Capt. Rafferty and Officer Franklin. Rafferty is holding a package. Steve takes a picture of the men. Then he waits and listens.

"So Tyrone, do we have a deal?"

"I don't know, captain," says Tyrone in his thick Jamaican accent. "It's pretty steep."

"You won't find it any cheaper anywhere else."

"Besides," says Franklin, "it's not like we're taking your last dollar. You've got plenty."

"Okay, but let's get this over with, before someone sees us. After all, this is a public place."

"Don't worry, Tyrone. That's why I picked it. No one would think anything of it."

"Yeah," says Franklin. "They'd probably think we were questioning you about a case."

Tyrone hands Rafferty the briefcase. "It's all here." Steve photographs them. Then Rafferty hands Tyrone the package. Steve takes

14

another picture. He now has the whole transaction on film. "Weasel was right," he mutters silently. "This really is big." Steve decides it's time to leave before they see him, but just as he starts to leave, he steps on a branch and it makes a crackling noise.

"What was that?" asks Tyrone.

"I don't know," says Rafferty, "but we'd better check it out."

Steve starts to run, but Franklin spots him. "Look! There he is."

"Okay," says Rafferty, "You two go after him. I'll make around and catch him at the other end."

Franklin catches up with Steve and throws him to the ground. Tyrone catches up with them and they hold Steve until Rafferty arrives.

"Hey, what's going on here?" demands Steve.

Rafferty recognizes Steve. "I might ask you the same question, Mr. Marks."

Tyrone also recognizes Steve. "Hey, I know this cat. He's a reporter for the Gazette."

"An investigative reporter," adds Rafferty.

"I bet he saw everything."

"I didn't see anything."

Franklin notices the camera around Steve's neck. "Sure you did." He takes a handkerchief out of his pants pocket and lifts the camera from Steve's neck.. "Well just look at what I found. It looks like a camera."

"Damn!" exclaims Tyrone. "He even took pictures of us."

"Look! I don't know what you're talking about."

"Sure you do," says Rafferty. "This story will probably be on page one by tomorrow morning. You were probably on your way to get these pictures developed."

"It's too bad you won't get a chance to," retorts Franklin. He pulls the film out of the camera, thus exposing it. Then he drops the camera on the ground and smashes it with his feet. "Now that's the end of that."

"Mr. Marks, I bet you were even going to tell your old friend Harley about this."

"I told you I don't know what you're talking about."

"So you still want to play dumb."

"What are we going to do with him?" asks Franklin.

"Well, we'll just have to take care of this snoop."

Fearing for his life, Steve tries to bargain with them. "Hey, why don't you just let me go. I promise I won't say anything."

Rafferty lets out a high pitched laugh. "Mr. Marks, I see you've just regained your memory. It doesn't matter, because we're going to make sure you never say another word to anyone ever again."

Rafferty's statement disturbs Tyrone. "Hey, I don't want to be involved in a murder."

"You already are, Tyrone." Rafferty takes a pair of black leather gloves out of his coat pocket and puts them on. He then takes a switchblade out of his pants pocket.

A look of fear comes over Steve's face. He tries unsuccessfully to break free from Tyrone and Franklin. "You won't get away with this."

Rafferty stabs Steve in the abdomen. Steve clutches his abdomen and falls to the ground fatally wounded. "I already have." He takes off the gloves and puts them back in his pocket. "Come on. Let's get out of here."

They all leave the park. About a minute later, Jessup comes walking through the park. He is lighting a cigarette when he spots Steve's body. He moves a little closer to get a better view. As he leans over, he unknowingly drops his matchbook. "Hey, fella, you had too much to drink?" No response. So he rolls the body over and notices the blade in Steve's abdomen. Then he looks at Steve's face and a look of recognition comes over his face. "Oh, my God."

Suddenly an octogenarian, walking a brown and white collie, arrives on the scene. He sees Jessup kneeling by the body. "Hey, what's going on here?" When Jessup sees him, he panics and runs away. "Hey, come back here." Jessup keeps on running. The old man kneels by Steve's body, while his dog sniffs it. "Young man, are you okay?" He feels for a pulse, but there isn't any. "Chip, you stay here while I go call the police." Chip barks. Old man leaves.

Ten minutes later, the crime scene is sealed off. Franklin is on the scene when Rafferty and Harley arrive.

"So what have you got, Franklin?"

"A black man with a fatal stab wound to the abdomen."

"Any I.D.?" asks Harley.

"I'm afraid so." The urgent look on Franklin's face indicates something is wrong.

"Well, who is it, Franklin?"

"It's your friend Steve Marks."

17

"Steve." Harley, pushing Franklin aside, goes up and kneels by the body. He is shocked to see his best friend lying in a pool of blood. "Oh Steve."

Rafferty looks slyly at Franklin. "I'm sorry about your friend, Harley."

"Yeah, so am I."

"He was a reporter for the Gazette. Do you know what story he was working on? Maybe there's a connection?"

"No. But he must've been working on something, because he was supposed to meet a contact later. At least that's what he told me earlier."

"You mean you saw him earlier?"

"Yeah. He came over for Stacy's birthday. He said he was meeting a contact, but he didn't say who."

"Maybe that's the person who killed him."

"Maybe."

"Were there any witnesses?"

"Yes, captain. This gentleman found the body." Points to the old man. Rafferty and Harley proceed to question the old man, while Franklin examines the crime scene.

"Sir, I'm Capt. Rafferty and this is Det. Jefferson. We'd like to ask you a couple of questions."

"Sure."

"I understand you found the body."

"Well, sort of."

"What do you mean by sort of?" asks Harley.

"Well, when I got here, there was another man kneeling by the body. He ran off when I saw him."

"What did he look like?"

"He was an average looking white man."

"Do you think you'll be able to identify this man if you saw him again?"

"I think so."

Suddenly Franklin comes upon the matchbook and broken camera. He takes out his handkerchief and picks up the items. Then he goes over to Rafferty and Harley. "Excuse me. Captain, I found these next to the body." He hands them to Rafferty.

Harley recognizes the camera. "That's Steve's camera. Obviously someone didn't want him taking their picture."

"I wonder if this matchbook belongs to him."

"Magnolia Lounge. Maybe the killer dropped it," says Harley.

"Maybe. Franklin, make sure the lab checks these and the murder weapon for prints."

"Sure, captain."

"Harley, do you feel like going to the Magnolia Lounge with me?"

"Sure, captain."

5

Rafferty and Harley arrive at the Magnolia Lounge. The bartender is standing behind the bar. Both men sit at the bar. The bartender notices them. "Gentlemen, what's your pleasure?"

They take out their badges. "Sorry, we're on duty."

"What do you cops want?"

"I'm Capt. Rafferty and this is Det. Jefferson."

"So what."

"We'd like to ask you a couple of questions."

"Look! I run a clean operation. I don't want to be hassled."

"We're not here to hassle you," says Harley. "We just want to ask you a couple of questions."

"Okay."

On the bar, Rafferty notices a tray with matchbooks identical to the one found near Steve Marks' body. "Are these the only matchbooks you have here?"

"Yes. They're for our customers."

"Do you know Steve Marks?" asks Harley.

"Yes, I know him. He's a regular. A real nice guy. Why? Is he in some sort of trouble?"

"He was found stabbed to death in the park tonight."

"What! I can't believe this. I just saw him earlier."

"You mean you saw him earlier," inquires Harley.

"Yes. He came in about eight."

"This must be where he went after he left my house."

"Was he alone?"

"Yes, but…"

"But what?"

"I don't know if this will help, but he got into a little scuffle with two white customers. I saw everything and none of it was his fault."

"Tell us what happened," says Harley.

"Well, Steve bumped into one of the fellas and he even apologized, but they started acting crazy."

"In what way?"

"Well, they started making a bunch of racist remarks."

"What did they look like?"

"One was average looking and the other one was husky with wavy hair and they were wearing blue jeans and blue jean jackets."

Rafferty and Harley glance at each other.

"Did you get their names?" asks Harley.

"The big guy's name was Jake. That's all I know."

"What time did they leave?"

"I don't know exactly, but it was sometime after nine."

"Did they return later?" asks Harley.

"No. I wish I could be more help. I really liked Steve. I hope you catch the guy who did this."

"We will."

Phone rings. Bartender answers. "Magnolia Lounge. Yeah, hold on. Captain, it's Officer Franklin."

"Thanks. Yeah, Franklin."

"Captain, there weren't any prints on the camera, but we did find a set on the matchbook."

"Whose are they?"

"Harold Jessup. He's staying at the Clarion Motel, room #2."

"What about the murder weapon?"

"Nothing. It was wiped clean."

"I want you to check all stores in town that sell switchblades. Find out if any were sold to anyone fitting Jessup or Spooner's description."

"I will, captain."

Rafferty hangs up. "The prints found on the matchbook belong to Harold Jessup. He's staying at the Clarion."

"Do you think he and Spooner could be involved in Steve's murder?"

"I hope not, Harley. That's all we need is a racially motivated murder."

"I think it's time we pay Harold Jessup a visit."

"So do I, Harley."

Jessup is in his motel room sitting on a beat up, old sofa and looking at a <u>Playboy</u> magazine. On the wall, behind him, is a large Confederate flag. In front of him is a coffee table with a bunch of magazines. A few feet away, against the wall, is a small color television. Suddenly Spooner comes into the room singing. "I found my thrill on blueberry hill." He now whistles the same tune.

"Jake, I have to talk to you."

Spooner joins Jessup on the sofa. "Yeah, what about?"

"I think I may be in trouble."

"What kind of trouble?"

"You remember I told you I was going to go for a walk."

"Yeah."

"Well, I went to the park."

"Did something happen in the park?"

"Yeah, I was walking in the park when I came upon this man lying on the ground. At first I thought he was drunk, so I moved a little closer to get a better look. That's when I saw he was dead. He had been stabbed."

"What!"

"That's not the half of it."

"You mean there's more?"

"Yes. That dead guy was the same guy we had that run in with earlier tonight at the lounge."

"That nigger. Are you sure?"

"I'm positive."

"Did anyone see you?"

"Yes."

"Who?"

"An old man walking a dog came along and saw me kneeling next to the body."

"What did you do?"

"I panicked and ran. He probably thinks I'm the killer."

"Did he get a good look at you?"

"I'm not sure. I don't think so."

"Let's hope that old man can't recognize you."

"It won't matter, not if I have an alibi."

"But you don't."

"You can be any alibi, Jake."

"What! You don't know what you're asking."

"I'm asking for your help."

"I can't. I was with Cindy. You know that. Besides, the cops might find out."

"Don't worry. They won't. So will you help me?"

"Okay, Okay."

Knock at the door. "Who is it?"

"Capt. Rafferty and Det. Jefferson. We'd like to ask you a couple of questions, Mr. Jessup."

Jessup and Spooner look at each other. Then Jessup gets up to open the door. "Well, captain, I didn't think I'd get a visit from you while I was in Clarion."

"I'm afraid this is official police business."

"Come in."

"Thank you." They enter. Spooner is still sitting on the sofa. "Oh, Mr. Spooner, I didn't see you over there."

"Captain." He flashes Harley a detestable look.

"Gentlemen, to what do we owe the pleasure of your company?"

"I understand that you and Mr. Spooner had an altercation with another man at the Magnolia earlier this evening."

"I wouldn't call it an altercation. It was more like a misunderstanding. Why? Is he pressing charges?"

"No," says Harley. "Steve Marks, that's his name, was found stabbed to death in the park tonight."

"Oh, that's terrible, but I don't understand what this has to do with us. We didn't kill him."

"No one said you did."

"No, you didn't," says Spooner, "but you think it. You think just because we're klansmen, who just happened to have had a misunderstanding with some nigger who just happens to turn up dead, we're automatically involved."

"He wasn't just some nigger. He was my best friend and my daughter's godfather."

"We don't give a shit who he was. We didn't kill him."

"Where were you tonight, Mr. Jessup?"

"Jake and I went to the Magnolia and then we came back here."

"Is that right, Mr. Spooner?" asks Harley.

"Yes, it is."

"That's what we've been telling you all along. We don't know anything."

"Well, you must know something, Mr. Jessup. A matchbook with your fingerprints on it was found next to the body. Could you explain how it got there?"

"How should I know? Maybe someone put it there."

"Who?" asks Harley.

"I don't know. Maybe it was someone who doesn't like me."

Rafferty looks at Harley and smiles. "Mr. Jessup, that could be anyone including myself and Det. Jefferson."

"What about you, Mr. Spooner? Do you have any idea how the matchbook got there?"

"Maybe the killer put it there."

"True, but how would the killer get the matchbook?"

"I don't know. Maybe he picked it up at the Magnolia and accidentally dropped it next to the body."

"Mr. Jessup," says Rafferty, "do you remember if you had the matchbook when you left the Magnolia?"

"No, I don't."

"Mr. Spooner," says Harley, "you referred to the killer as he. How did you know he was a man and not a woman?"

"I didn't. It was just a figure of speech."

"Well, I think that'll be all for now, but don't leave town. We may need to ask you some more questions. Good night, gentlemen." Rafferty and Harley walk out and stand in the hall outside the room. "Well, Harley, what do you think?"

"I think they're lying."

"So do I. Well, there's nothing more we can do tonight, so we might as well call it a night."

"Okay, captain, but this is the first time I'm not happy to be going home."

"Yeah, I know what you mean. I wouldn't want to be in your shoes for anything in the world."

Harley walks into the softly lit living room. "Honey, I'm home." He walks over to the sofa and stares at the print "Birds of Paradise" hanging on the wall, but the painting is the furthest thing from his mind. There are magazines on the sofa table and an identical brass lamp on each end table. The room is further enhanced by a plush, light blue carpet.

Presently Roz comes into the room. "Hi, honey, I thought I heard your voice."

He kisses her on the cheeks. "Hey, honey. Is Stacy still up?"

"Yes. I think she's upstairs."

"I need to talk to both of you."

She detects a note of urgency in his voice. "Okay, I'll get her." She goes to the end of the stairs and calls Stacy. "Stacy, come down here please."

"Okay, mom." The exuberant teenager comes bounding down the stairs. "What's wrong, mom?"

"Your father wants to talk to us."

"Okay." They go into the living room. Harley is sitting on the sofa. They join him. "Hi, daddy."

"Hi, honey."

"Harley, what did you want to talk to us about?"

"Roz, I don't even know where to begin."

"Did something happen, Harley?"

"I'm afraid so."

"What's wrong, daddy?"

"It's Steve."

"Steve."

"Harley, did something happen to Steve?"

"He was found stabbed to death in the park tonight."

"Oh, my God."

"Oh no," says Stacy. She starts crying and Harley comforts her.

"Oh, Stacy, I knew you'd take it hard."

"Harley, who would want to hurt Steve? He didn't have an enemy in the world."

"Well, apparently he did."

"Does the department have a suspect?"

"We are looking at one guy who may have been involved. I just hope he's not responsible for Steve's death, because if he is, there's going to be trouble in Clarion."

"What do you mean, Harley? Just who is this suspect?"

"He's a klansman."

"I should have guessed it would be a klansman. It's all over town about them marching on Saturday."

"Yeah. Everyone's talking about it at school. Plus it's all over the news."

"Why would he want to kill Steve?"

"He and Steve had an argument earlier tonight."

"Why hasn't he been arrested?"

"He has an alibi and even if he didn't, we don't have enough evidence to arrest him."

"He's probably going to figure out a way to beat the charges," says Stacy. "They always do."

"Harley, do you think he's guilty?"

"I don't know, Roz."

"Of course he's guilty," says Stacy. "He's a klansman."

6

Franklin is sitting at the front desk. Rafferty is sitting on the desk facing him.

"Captain, this might all blow up in our faces."

"Don't worry, Franklin. As long as we all keep our mouths shut, everything will be okay."

"What if Det. Jefferson finds out something. He really wants to find his friend's killer."

"Don't worry. He won't. Besides, he thinks Jessup did it."

At this moment, Harley walks in. "Good morning, everyone."

"Good morning, Harley."

"Good morning, Det. Jefferson."

"Captain, any leads on the case?"

"No, Harley, nothing new. By the way, how are Roz and Stacy doing?"

"Well, they took it pretty hard, but they're going to be okay."

"I'm glad, Harley. Harley, if you feel you're too close to the case, I can assign you to another case or I can even arrange for you to take some time off to spend with your family."

"I appreciate that, captain, but I'd rather stay on the case and try to find out who killed Steve."

"Okay, Harley.

Phone rings. Franklin answers. "Clarion police, Officer Franklin speaking."

"This is the bartender from the Magnolia. I'd like to speak to Capt. Rafferty."

"Hold on. Captain, it's the bartender from the Magnolia. He wants to speak to you."

"Okay. Put him on the speaker."

Franklin presses on the intercom.

"Capt. Rafferty speaking."

"Captain, last night I forgot to mention that there was a woman with Jessup and Spooner."

"Did you know her?"

"Yes. She's a regular. Name's Cindy James."

"Did she leave with them?"

"I watched them leave together."

"Interesting, very interesting. You wouldn't happen to know her address."

"110 Fifth Street."

"Thank you, sir."

Bartender hangs up. Franklin turns off the intercom.

"Harley, I think we'd better go see what this young lady knows."

"Captain, I'm right behind."

They arrive at Cindy James' house. They go up to the front door and Rafferty knocks. Cindy answers from inside. "Who is it?"

"It's the police, Miss James."

She opens the door. "Yes."

"I"m Capt. Rafferty and this is Det. Jefferson."

"Come in." They step into the brightly decorated living room. "What can I do for you?"

"We'd like to ask you a couple of questions," says Harley.

"About what?"

"Harold Jessup and Jake Spooner," says Rafferty. "I understand you know them."

"Yes. I met them at the Magnolia Lounge, but how did you know?"

"The bartender told us," says Harley.

"Well, if the bartender already told you, then why are you here? Are they in some sort of trouble?"

"We're not sure," says Harley. "Did you know that prior to meeting you, they had a run in with another customer?"

"No I didn't, but I'm sure it was all just a misunderstanding."

"Well, I don't know about that," says Rafferty. "The guy they had the run in with was found stabbed to death in the park last night."

"What."

"The bartender said you left with them," says Harley.

"Not exactly. I walked out with them, but Jake and I left together."

"How long were you together?" asks Rafferty.

"At least a couple hours."

"What about Jessup?" asks Harley.

"He said he was going for a walk and then head back to the motel."

"Thank you, Miss James," says Rafferty. "You've been a lot of help. Good day."

"Good day, gentlemen."

31

They leave Cindy's house and get into the brown Chevrolet Impala parked outside. Rafferty gets in the driver's seat. "So Jessup doesn't have an alibi after all."

"Sure looks that way."

"He could be our man."

"I know."

Rafferty gets on the police radio and calls Franklin at the station. Franklin's voice comes through on the police radio. "Yeah, captain."

"Franklin, I want you to call that old man from the park and tell him to come to the station as soon as possible. Also, pick up Jessup and Spooner and bring them in for questioning."

"Okay, captain. Oh, captain, I almost forgot. I checked every store that sells switchblades."

"So what did you find out?"

"I talked to store owners and employees. No one remembers anyone fitting Jessup or Spooner's description who bought a switchblade recently."

"Okay, Franklin. We're on our way to the Gazette, then on to the morgue. We'll meet you at the station in about one hour."

"Okay, captain."

Rafferty hangs up. "It's looks like we won't be able to tie Jessup or Spooner to the murder weapon after all."

"That's too bad. Well, let's just hope that old man can make a positive I.D. If not, I'm afraid we don't have a case."

"You're right, Harley."

Rafferty and Harley arrive at the office of the managing editor of the <u>Clarion Gazette</u>. Rafferty knocks on the door. The voice of Harry O'Neal comes booming through the door. "Come in." The pot bellied O'Neal, with a receding hairline, is sitting at a messy desk. He glances above his gold rimmed glasses as the two policemen enter his office.

"Mr. O'Neal, I'm Capt. Rafferty and this is Det. Jefferson. We'd like to ask you a couple questions about Steve Marks."

"Sure. Please sit down." They sit. "Jefferson. Are you related to Stacy Jefferson?"

"Yes. She's my daughter."

"Steve talked about his goddaughter all the time. He was very proud of her."

"Yes, I know. She was also very proud of him."

"You know he was the best damn reporter I've ever had the pleasure of working with."

"Mr. O'Neal, did you know what story he was working on? Maybe there's a connection to his murder."

"No, I didn't. I've looked through his desk to see if he left behind any clues as to what he was working on. So far nothing."

"Was it unusual not to let anyone in on what he was working on?"

"No, not for an investigative reporter. Steve usually kept everything under wraps, at least until he was ready to break the story."

"Did he have any contacts?" asks Harley.

"I'm sure he did, but a reporter's contacts are confidential."

"Do you know of any stories he'd done in the past which may have led to his murder?" asks Harley.

33

"I can't think of any."

"Thank you, Mr. O'Neal. If you think of anything else, please let us know."

"I will."

"Good day, Mr. O'Neal."

"Good day, gentlemen."

Rafferty and Harley enter the cold, gloomy county morgue. There are at least half a dozen stiffs, covered by white sheets, lying on gurneys. One is Steve Marks. There is a thick, white towel with various instruments commonly used for autopsies on top of a small, metal, rollaway table near Steve's body. Standing near the table is the meticulous county coroner, Dr. Brad Johnson. He has just completed the autopsy on Steve's body when Rafferty and Harley arrive. "Hello, gentlemen. I was expecting you."

"Well, Doc, I hope this means that you've completed the autopsy on Steve Marks."

"As a matter of fact, I just finished."

"So what can you tell us?" asks Harley.

"A single stab wound to the lower abdomen. Death was instantaneous."

"What was the approximate time of death?"

"The approximate time of death was somewhere between nine thirty and ten."

"Anything else?" asks Harley.

"Yes. His heart was pretty agitated."

"What could have caused this?"

"Any kind of exertion, such as exercising, jogging or running."

"Maybe he was running away from something or someone," says Harley.

"Yeah. That would explain the irregular heart rhythm."

"Is that all?"

"Not quite. Come closer. Take a look at these bruises on the victim's arms."

The policemen examine the bruises which are of a dark bluish color. "What could have caused these bruises?" asks Rafferty.

"It seems that someone may have been holding his arms very tight."

"The killer?" asks Harley.

"Yeah. The victim may have tried to get away and the assailant may have grabbed his arms to prevent him from escaping. Or…"

"Or there may have had another assailant," adds Rafferty.

"One who held him while the other one stabbed him," says Harley.

"Of course I can't say for sure that there were two assailants. It's just a theory."

"Can you tell us anything more?"

"I'm afraid not."

"If you think of anything else," adds Harley, "please let us know."

"I will."

"Good day."

"Good day, gentlemen."

7

Harley is seated in the interrogation room with Jessup and Spooner, while Rafferty is standing outside in the hall waiting for Franklin. Presently Franklin comes up. "Captain, the old man from the park is here."

"Bring him in." Franklin goes around the corner and returns with the old man. The old man stands next to Rafferty facing a glass window. "Now, sir" says Rafferty, "just look right in this window and tell me if you see the man you saw kneeling next to Steve Marks' body. Don't worry. He can't see you. It's a one way mirror."

The old man looks at the two men sitting next to Harley. He looks at Jessup, then at Spooner, then back at Jessup.

"Yeah, that's him. The guy on the left." He identifies Jessup. "I would recognize him anywhere."

"Thank you, sir. That'll be all for now. If we need you again, we'll call you."

"Sure, captain."

"Officer Franklin will show you out." Franklin leaves with him. Rafferty joins the others in the interrogation room. "Gentlemen, glad you could join us."

"It's not like we had a choice," says Spooner. "Your officer picked us up and brought us here like a bunch of common criminals."

"Why are we here?" asks Jessup.

"We told you we didn't know anything," adds Spooner.

"Well, Mr. Spooner, that's not quite true," says Rafferty.

"We spoke to Cindy James," says Harley. Spooner glances at Jessup in an I told you so fashion. "She told us she was with you during the time of Steve Marks' murder. Is that true?"

"Yes."

"So you lied to protect your friend," says Rafferty.

"Yes."

"Mr. Jessup, I'm afraid we're going to have to place you under arrest."

"What for?"

"For the murder of Steve Marks. Harley, read him his rights."

"Mr. Jessup, you have the right to remain silent. Anything you say can and will be used against you in a court of law. You have the right to an attorney. If you cannot afford one, one will be provided for you at no cost. Do you understand your rights?"

"Yeah, I understand."

"Would you like to have an attorney present before we question you?" asks Harley.

"I'll get an attorney later. Right now I just want to answer your questions."

"Okay."

"Mr. Jessup, were you in the park last night? Before you answer, I want you to know that a witness just identified you as the man kneeling next to Steve Marks' body."

"Yes, I was there, but I didn't kill him."

"Tell us what happened?"

37

"I was walking in the park, when I noticed this man lying on the ground. I went closer to get a better look and that's when I saw he was dead."

"Did you recognize the dead man?" asks Harley.

"Yes. He was the same guy Jake and I had that run in with earlier that night at the Magnolia."

"What happened next?" asks Rafferty.

"Then along comes this old man walking a dog."

"What did you do?" asks Harley.

"I ran. That must be when I dropped my matchbook."

"Why did you run away if you were innocent?" asks Rafferty.

"I was afraid, so I panicked."

"Why did you lie about being in the park?" asks Rafferty.

"Because no one would have believed me. A klansman finds a dead black guy. Now would you have believed me if I said I was innocent? No, you wouldn't have. That's why I lied. I didn't kill Steve Marks. I swear."

"That may be, Mr. Jessup," says Harley, "but we have enough evidence to arrest you. You had an altercation with the victim prior to his murder. Your matchbook was found next to the body. Plus, our witness places you at the scene of the murder."

"That's just circumstantial evidence."

"If you're as innocent as you say you are," adds Rafferty, "then you'll have a chance to prove it in a court of law."

"Are there any questions?" asks Harley.

"No questions," replies Jessup.

"Well, let's all go to the front desk. Mr. Jessup, I'll have Franklin take you to the back for fingerprinting and processing." They head to the front and find Franklin standing there talking to a group of black men. Warren Brooks, carrying a dark gray briefcase, is their leader. "Franklin, who are all these people?"

"They're from the NAACP and they want to talk to you?"

"Oh, Jesus, just what I need." He proceeds to address the group. "I'm Capt. Rafferty and this is Det. Jefferson. What can we do for you gentlemen?"

"I'm Warren Brooks, director of the local NAACP and a member of your town council."

"We already know who you are, Mr. Brooks," says Rafferty. "We just want to know what you're doing here."

"We're here because we heard that the Klan is responsible for the death of Steve Marks."

"That's a damn lie, nigger," shouts Spooner.

Brooks lunges at Spooner and grabs him by the collar. "You white bastard."

Harley and Franklin separate both men. "Hey, break it off," says Harley.

"Gentlemen, I won't stand for this kind of behavior in my station. Is that clear?" Both men nod their heads. "Franklin, please take Mr. Jessup to the back and have him fingerprinted and processed."

"Yes, captain."

"Mr. Spooner," continues Rafferty, "if you want to accompany your friend, you may. Otherwise, I would appreciate if you just leave."

"I'm leaving, but first I'd like to have a moment with my friend."

"Go ahead."

Spooner and Jessup move over to the side and talk among themselves. "Hey, buddy, you're going to need a lawyer."

"Yeah, I know. I guess I never thought it would come to this."

"Well, it has and there's nothing we can do to change it. Meanwhile, I'm going to see about finding you a good criminal lawyer. I'll try to find one before the arraignment."

"Okay. Thanks, Jake. I owe you one."

"Don't mention it. Take care."

"I will."

Spooner leaves and Franklin takes Jessup to the back. Rafferty and Harley remain standing with Brooks and the other gentlemen. "As for you, Mr. Brooks," says Rafferty, "if you are going to come in here and stir up trouble, then you might just as well leave, too."

"I won't leave until I say what I've come to say," says a very determined Brooks.

"Okay, we're listening."

"Captain, a very well respected member of the black community was murdered. We're here to make sure that justice is done and that nothing is swept under the carpet."

"Mr. Brooks, I assure you that nothing has been swept under the carpet."

"Mr. Brooks, Steve Marks was my best friend and I promise you that we will do everything humanly possible to make sure that the person or persons responsible are brought to justice."

"I was under the impression you had the person responsible."

"Yes, we have, Mr. Brooks," says Rafferty, "but if it turns out this man is innocent, I'll release him. I won't keep an innocent man in jail just to please your organization. I know you wouldn't want that either, Mr. Brooks."

"No, I wouldn't, captain. Well, I think I've said just about everything I came to say. Good day, gentlemen."

"Good day, Mr. Brooks."

Brooks and his group leave. Rafferty and Harley are still standing at the front desk when Franklin returns.

"Captain, Mr. Jessup has been processed and taken to lock up."

"Good, Franklin."

"Det. Jefferson, Mr. Jessup would like to speak to you."

"To me! What about?"

"He didn't say."

"Thanks, Franklin." Harley leaves.

"Franklin, do you think Jessup knows anything about what went down in the park?"

"I doubt it. He was just in the wrong place at the wrong time."

"Yeah and lucky for us he was. We've got a good thing going, Franklin. No one suspects anything and I won't allow anyone to spoil it. So make sure you keep a close eye on him."

"I will, captain. What about Spooner?"

"I don't think he knows anything. Jessup is the only one we have to worry about."

Jessup is sitting on a small cot in his cell. The cell also contains a toilet and a face bowl. Harley arrives to talk to Jessup. He stands outside the cell. Jessup gets up from his cot and stands face to face with Harley.

"Franklin said you wanted to talk to me."

"Yeah, I do."

"What do you want to talk to me about?"

"Det. Jefferson, do you believe I killed your friend?" Harley doesn't answer. "You do, don't you?"

"Yeah, I do."

"Well, here's a news flash for you. I didn't do it. I may be a lot of things, including a racist, but I'm not a murderer."

"You say that so sincerely, I almost want to believe you, but I know what your kind are capable of. So cut the crap. I'm not buying it."

"That's too bad, because your friend's murderer is still out there. You know what's wrong with you, Jefferson?"

"No, I don't know what's wrong with me, Jessup. So why don't you just enlighten me?"

"I will, but you won't like it."

"Let me be the judge of that."

"You're letting the fact that I'm a klansman cloud your judgement. Maybe I'm not the only racist here."

Harley is so incensed by his statement, he can hardly speak. "Don't...Don't you ever call me a racist."

"The truth hurts, doesn't it, Jefferson?"

"Jessup, I'm going to walk out of here before I do something I may regret." Still furious, Harley walks out.

8

Spooner enters the spacious office of Mitchell Delaney, a hard nosed attorney with a top notch reputation. Delaney stands and shakes hands with Spooner. "Mr. Spooner, please sit down."

"Thank you, Mr. Delaney. I'm glad you were able to see me on such short notice."

"Well, Mr. Spooner, it sounded very urgent on the phone."

"It is."

"So how can I help you, Mr. Spooner?"

"I need an attorney for a friend of mine."

Delaney takes a legal pad and a pen out of the desk drawer. "What's your friend's name?"

"Harold Jessup."

"What kind of trouble is he in?"

"He's been arrested and charged with murder."

"Whose murder has he been charged with?"

"A reporter by the name of Steve Marks."

Delaney raises his eyebrows at the mention of Steve Marks' name. "Steve Marks! Mr. Spooner, is your friend a klansman?"

"Yes. So am I, but how did you know?"

"This is a small town, Mr. Spooner. Word travels fast."

"It sure does. I hope that won't stop you from representing my friend. He's innocent and he needs a good lawyer."

"Don't worry. I'll still represent him, but I need to talk to him before the arraignment."

"His arraignment is set for this afternoon."

Delaney looks at his watch. "I'll try to head over there during my lunch break."

"Thank you, Mr. Delaney."

"Don't mention it. Well, I think that's all the questions I have. If I think of anymore, I'll ask Mr. Jessup when I see him. Mr. Spooner, I'll see you at the arraignment. Good day."

"Good day, Mr. Delaney."

Delaney is sitting at a table in the police station conference room. Suddenly the door opens. Franklin comes in followed by Jessup. "I'll leave you two alone."

"Thank you, officer." Franklin leaves. Jessup sits in the only other chair available. "Mr. Jessup, I'm Mitchell Delaney, your attorney. Your friend Jake Spooner came to see me."

"Thanks for coming."

"Mr. Jessup, your friend told me of your situation. Now I want you to tell me everything that happened the night of the murder."

"Well, I was walking through the park when I came upon this man lying on the ground. At first I thought he was drunk or asleep, so I moved a little closer to get a better look. That's when I saw he was dead. He had been stabbed."

"What happened next?"

"Then this old man with a dog comes along and sees me."

"What did you do?"

"I panicked and ran."

"Why did you run?"

"I was afraid."

"Did you know the dead man?"

"Yes. He was the same guy Jake and I had a run in with earlier that night at the Magnolia."

"What kind of run in?"

"When Jake and I were arriving, this guy was walking out and he bumped into me."

"Steve Marks?"

"Yeah, I didn't find out his name until later."

"Go on."

"Like I said he bumped into me. It was an accident and he even apologized."

"I don't understand. If he apologized, then how did the trouble start?"

"I'm afraid that was me and Jake's fault."

"How so?"

"After he apologized, I made a remark, then Jake made a remark and pretty soon everything got out of control."

"What kind of remarks?"

"Racial remarks."

"I see."

"I don't know why I did that. As I look back on it, I realized how stupid it was."

"Did anyone else see what happened?"

"Yeah, the bartender and I guess some of the patrons. Why?"

"Maybe the killer was following Steve and overheard you and him arguing."

"Maybe."

"He knew you would be blamed for the murder, because you had argued with Steve in full view of the bartender and the other patrons."

"You've got a point there, Mr. Delaney, but something still puzzles me."

"Yeah. What' s that, Mr. Jessup?"

"If the killer was following Steve, like you say, then how could he know I would be in the park that night?"

"He didn't. Your being in the park was just a coincidence which happened to work to his advantage."

"Boy, talk about bad timing."

"Of course there's another possibility."

"I'm almost afraid to ask what it is."

"Maybe you were just in the wrong place at the wrong time."

"Either way I'm in trouble."

"I'm afraid so, Mr. Jessup."

"You really believe me, don't you?"

"Yes, I do."

Jessup breathes a sigh of relief. "Besides Jake, you're the only other person who believes me."

"Your arraignment is set for this afternoon."

"Yes. At four o'clock."

"At that time the judge will set bail. Will you be able to post it?"

"Yes. I think so."

"Okay. I'll meet you at the courtroom for the arraignment."

"Thank you, Mr. Delaney."

Jessup is being arraigned on charges of first degree murder. Seated at the table on the left are Rafferty and Harley, along with Ed Rollins, the fresh, young, eager district attorney itching to make a name for himself. Delaney, Jessup and Spooner are seated at the table on the right. Judge Raines, a, middle aged woman with a learned expression, is seated on the bench. A gavel is on her right. "People vs Harold Jessup. Are all the parties present?"

Rollins and Delaney stand up.

"We are, your honor," says Rollins.

"Yes, your honor," says Delaney.

"Present your evidence, Mr. Rollins."

"Thank you, your honor. The prosecution is prepared to prove that Mr. Jessup had a motive for murdering Steve Marks."

"What motive?"

"Hate."

"Please explain."

"We all know that the defendant is a klansman."

"Does this have anything to do with your case?"

"Yes, your honor."

"Proceed."

"Your honor, prior to the murder, Mr. Jessup and his friend had an altercation with the deceased at the Magnolia Lounge. Mr. Jessup and his friend made a couple of racial remarks."

"Were there any witnesses to this incident?"

"Yes, there were several witnesses and one of them, the bartender, is prepared to testify that Mr. Jessup and his friend instigated the whole incident."

"Go on."

"Mr. Jessup's matchbook was found next to the body. Also, we have a witness that places him at the scene of the murder."

"Is there anymore evidence to present?"

"That's it, your honor."

"Mr. Delaney, do you have anything to add?"

"Yes, your honor."

"Proceed."

"Your honor, all of the evidence that Mr. Rollins just presented is circumstantial. Mr. Jessup is just a victim of being in the wrong place at the wrong time."

"After hearing all the evidence, I'm prepared to set bail at fifty thousand dollars."

"Your honor, I object."

"Mr. Rollins, my decision is final. Mr. Delaney, will your client be able to post bail?"

"Yes, your honor."

"Mr. Jessup, after you post bail, you are free until the trial. Don't leave town. If you jump bail, you will be apprehended and charged with evading trial and unlawful flight. You will then remain in jail until your trial. Is that understood, Mr. Jessup?"

Jessup stands. "Yes, your honor."

"Any questions?"

"None, your honor," says Delaney.

"No questions," says Rollins.

"Court is adjourned." She bangs the gavel.

9

Jessup is sitting on the sofa in his motel room eating pepperoni pizza, drinking a beer and watching TV. Spooner comes out of the bathroom. "I'm going to the lobby to get a paper. Need anything?"

"No."

"Okay, I'll be right back."

Spooner leaves and closes the door behind him. Suddenly the door reopens. "Hey, did you forget something?" No answer. "Jake, didn't you hear me?" Still no answer. So Jessup turns around and sees two strange men, with stockings on their faces and wearing black leather gloves, standing in the doorway. "Who are you?" They don't answer. Instead they walk toward him. He backs away. "Look! I don't know who you are or what you want, but you'd better leave before I call the cops." They keep coming. Then one grabs Jessup and holds him, while the other one proceeds to beat him. "Hey, what's going on here?" He hits Jessup in the mouth with his right fist, busting his bottom lip. Then he gives him a right knee to the stomach and a right elbow to the back. Jessup, holding his stomach, falls to the floor in pain. The one who held him speaks.

"You'd better keep quiet about that murder in the park. If you saw anything, don't breathe a word to the cops or you're a dead man."

Although the muffled voice is unknown to him, Jessup can tell the man has an accent. "I don't know what you're talking about."

"That's more like it. Come on, man. Let's get out of here."

As they are about to leave, Spooner returns. "Hey, what's going on here?" He drops his newspaper and jumps one of the men. The other one pulls him off and throws him to the floor. As he falls, he fatally hits his head on the corner of the coffee table.

Before going out the door, one man removes his stocking. Vision blurred, Jessup can barely make out his face, but he does recognize him as none other than Officer Jeff Franklin. "Officer Franklin!" Jessup, in shock, crawls over to his friend. "Jake, are you okay?" He lifts Spooner by the shoulders and notices a pool of blood on the floor beneath his head. He feels for a pulse. None. "Oh, my God." He then crawls over to the phone and dials.

"Hello. Jefferson residence," answers Stacy.

"I want to speak to Det. Jefferson."

"Hold on. Daddy, it's for you."

Harley comes to the phone. "Who is it, Stacy?"

"Some guy."

She hands him the receiver. "Hello."

"Jefferson."

"Yeah. Who is this?"

"It's Jessup."

"What do you want, Jessup?"

"I'm at my motel room. Two men broke in. They beat me and Jake. I think Jake's dead."

"What! I'll call Capt. Rafferty and we'll be right over."

"No. Come alone. I'll explain. Please, Jefferson."

"Okay, Jessup. I'll be right there."

51

"Thanks."

Harley hangs up. "Roz, I have to go out for a minute."

"Okay, be careful," hollers Roz from the kitchen.

"I will."

Harley arrives at Jessup's motel room. Jessup, in severe pain, clutching his stomach, is kneeling on the floor next to Spooner's body. His face is bruised and his mouth is bleeding. "Are you okay?"

"Well, I've had better days."

"Let's get you over to the sofa." Harley puts his right arm around Jessup's waist and Jessup puts his left arm around Harley's neck. Slowly, they make it to the sofa. Then Harley goes into the bathroom to get a damp cloth to wipe Jessup's mouth.

"Ouch." Their eyes meet. "Thanks for coming."

"Sure." He gives the cloth to Jessup, while he examines Spooner's body.

"Jake's dead, isn't he?"

"I'm afraid so. Tell me what happened?"

"Two guys with stockings on their faces and wearing gloves burst in here. They beat and threatened me."

"Why?"

"It had something to do with your friend's murder."

"What!"

"Only one spoke."

"What did he say?"

"He told me if I knew anything about that murder in the park, for me to keep quiet or I'd be a dead man."

"Did you recognize the voice?"

"No, but he had an accent."

"What kind of accent?"

"I don't know. It all happened so fast. So now do you believe that I had nothing to do with your friend's murder?"

"'Yeah, I believe you. Did he say anything else?"

"No. That was it."

"So someone out there is getting nervous. They probably think you saw the murder."

"I didn't. I arrived after the murder."

"Yeah, but they don't know that. Now where was Spooner when all this was going on?"

"He had just stepped out for a minute to get a newspaper."

"They were probably watching the room to see when he left. That's when they made their move."

"You've got a point there."

"So what happened next?"

"Well, when Jake returned and saw what was going on, he jumped one of the guys. Then the other one pulled him off and threw him to the floor. As he fell, his head hit the corner of the coffee table. He died instantly. I wish we had never come to this town. Then maybe Jake would still be alive." Harley goes over to the phone. "Who are you calling?"

"I'm calling the captain to let him know what happened. He'll probably assign you police protection."

"I don't want police protection."

"Why? Your life may be in danger. We can protect you."

"Can you protect me from cops?"

"Cops. What are you talking about?.."

"I'm talking about the guys who beat me and killed Jake."

"Are you trying to say that these guys were cops?"

"That's exactly what I'm saying."

"How do you know?

"Because I saw."

"I don't understand. I thought you said they were wearing stockings on their faces."

"They were, but as they were leaving, one removed his stocking."

"Did you recognize him?"

"Yes."

"Well, who was he?"

"Officer Franklin."

"Jeff Franklin! Are you sure it was him?"

"I'm positive."

"Are you saying that one of my best rookies may be involved in this?"

"That's exactly what I'm saying and I don't think he's the only one, either. There may be others and not just rookies."

"That's why you didn't want me to call Capt. Rafferty right away, but why did you call me? I'm a cop, too."

"Because you don't look like the kind of guy who would be involved in their own best friend's murder."

"Thanks for the vote of confidence, but something still puzzles me?"

"What's that?"

"Why would the police be involved in Steve's murder?"

"Wasn't he an investigative reporter?"

"Yeah, but what does that have to do with the police?"

"Maybe he was doing a story on police corruption."

"Police corruption in Clarion? No way."

"Whether they are or aren't corrupt, I still don't want them protecting me."

"So what are you going to do? They may come back."

"Well, I've got an idea."

"I'm almost afraid to ask what it is."

"We both want to find our friends' killer and prove my innocence at the same time."

"True."

"So why don't we work together?"

"I can't believe I'm hearing this."

"I can't believe I'm saying it."

"Are you sure you want to do this?"

"Yes. So what do you think?"

"Well, it's not a bad idea. Of course everything has to be done legally, nothing illegal. Remember I'm the cop and I call the shots."

"Fair enough."

"Do you have someone you can stay with, at least until this case is solved?"

"I don't know anyone in town."

"After we've finished here, put some stuff together. You can stay at my place."

"I can't believe I'm hearing this."

"I can't believe I'm saying it."

"Thanks, Jefferson."

"My wife will probably kill me." He goes over to the phone. "Well, I'd better call the captain and have some guys come in and dust for prints."

"Don't bother. They were wearing gloves."

"It doesn't matter. Some clues even gloves can't hide." He picks up the receiver. "We won't mention anything about Franklin, at least until we have enough proof."

"Sure."

Harley dials the phone.

Ten minutes later, Rafferty, Franklin and a couple of other officers converge on the scene. Some dust for prints, while another takes pictures of the crime scene. Rafferty and Franklin are both shocked to see that Spooner is dead. "Harley, what have you got?"

"Two men with stockings on their faces and wearing gloves broke in. He was beaten and his friend was killed."

"Well, Mr. Jessup, looks like trouble seems to follow you everywhere.

"Well, captain, I didn't ask for it, if that's what you mean."

"I didn't mean anything by it. It was just an observation."

"Captain, I know you don't like me, and I don't particularly care for you, either. So why don't you just keep your observations to yourself."

56

Both men stare intensely at each other. "So what did these two men say?"

"Only one spoke."

"What did he say?"

"He said if I knew anything about that murder in the park, for me to keep quiet or I'd be a dead man."

Rafferty glances over at Franklin and now realizes that he and Tyrone were those two men. "Did you recognize the voice?"

"No, but he had an accent."

"What kind of accent?"

"I don't know."

"Anything else?"

"That's it. So what are you going to do about this?"

"There's not much we can do. After all, you didn't see their faces."

"Maybe not, but they're probably the ones who killed that reporter."

"We don't have proof of that."

"Because you're not looking for proof. You already have a scapegoat."

"Look, Mr. Jessup, we'll check it out. That's about all we can do. In the meantime, I can assign you police protection."

"Captain, he can stay with me. I'll keep an eye on him."

"Harley, are you sure you want to do this?"

"Yes."

"Okay. Well, I think that's about it. Mr. Jessup, if something comes up, I'll contact you at Harley's."

"Okay."

Everyone has left the motel, except for Rafferty and Franklin who are standing outside. "You and Tyrone were responsible for what happened here tonight?"

"Yes, captain."

"What were you two thinking?"

"We just wanted to see if Jessup knew anything."

"How? By beating it out of him and killing his friend."

"It was an accident. Spooner came back while we were still here. He jumped Tyrone, so I grabbed him and pushed him to the floor. I didn't think he was dead."

"That's what's wrong with you, Franklin. You don't think. A mistake like that could cost us everything."

"I'm sorry, captain."

"It's too late for that. We have to be very careful from now on. I don't have a good feeling about Jessup. What really puzzles me is Harley bringing a klansman into his home. It's the most bizarre thing I've ever heard of and so unlike Harley."

"Do you think they know more than they're saying?"

"I don't know, but you'd better keep a close eye on them. Make sure they don't get too close."

"I will, captain."

10

Harley and Jessup arrive at the Jefferson house. They go inside. "Wait in here while I go talk to Roz."

"Okay."

Harley heads toward the kitchen, while Jessup goes into the living room and sits on the sofa. Presently, Stacy comes into the room carrying Jamie. "Oh. I didn't know we had company. Hi. I'm Stacy Jefferson and this is my little brother Jamie."

"Hi. I'm Harold Jessup."

"Nice to meet you, Mr. Jessup."

"Nice to meet both of you."

"Are you waiting for my dad?"

"Yes, I am."

They sit on the sofa next to him. Stacy stares at him. "Forgive me for staring, but what happened to your face?"

"I got into a little scuffle."

"My dad says we should always walk away from a fight."

"He's right."

"Have we met before?"

"No. I don't think so. Why?"

"Because you look so familiar."

"Well, they say we all have a twin somewhere in the world. Maybe you saw him."

"Maybe."

Roz is washing dishes when Harley walks into the kitchen. "Hi, baby." He kisses her on the cheek.

"Hi, honey. Where did you go off so quickly?"

"It was an emergency."

"You'd think I'd get used to being a cop's wife by now, but I haven't. I worry every time you walk out that door until I see you walk back in."

"Yeah, I know you do, but I'll be okay."

"So how's the investigation going?"

"We made an arrest."

"Oh, that's great, Harley. Is it that klansman?"

"Yeah," says a doubtful Harley.

"What's the matter, Harley? You don't sound very happy about the arrest. Don't you believe he's guilty?"

"At first I did, but not anymore."

"What happened to make you change your mind?"

"He was the one who called just before I left."

"I thought he had been arrested."

"Yeah, but he made bail."

"So what did he want?"

"He wanted me to come over to his motel room."

"Why?"

"Because earlier tonight two men with stockings on their faces and wearing gloves broke into his room. He was beaten and his friend was killed."

"Oh, my God. That's so horrible. I, myself, hate the idea of anybody being beaten or killed. I don't care if they are klansmen or not. It's just not right."

"I couldn't agree with you more."

"Was this in retaliation for Steve's murder?"

"At first that's what I thought."

"But you don't anymore."

"That's right."

"Why?"

"Because that klansman told me what one of those men said."

"And what was that?"

"One of the men told him that if he knew anything about Steve's murder for him to keep his mouth shut or he'd be a dead man."

"So Steve's killer is still out there?"

"I'm afraid so."

"Is the department dropping the charges against this man?"

"We don't have enough proof to drop the charges."

"Do you think you'll be able to find Steve's killer?"

"Yeah. With Jessup's help, I think we'll be able to."

"Who's Jessup? I've never heard of him. Is he new to the force?"

"He's not a cop."

"He's your snitch."

"No."

"Then who is this Jessup?"

"He's the suspect."

A look of shock comes over Roz's face. "The suspect! You must be joking."

"I'm not."

"You work with a klansman. I'll have to see it to believe it."

"Well, you can see it tonight."

"Harley, what are you talking about?"

"Honey, he's here."

"Where?"

"In the living room."

"In the living room! In this house?"

"Yeah."

"Harley, what's he doing here?"

"I think he may be in danger, so I told him he could stay with us."

"You didn't."

"I did."

"Honey, he can't stay with us. We have young children. Besides, there are other cops who can protect him. White cops."

"Yeah, I know, but he trusts me and I trust him."

"I never thought I would live to see the day when a klansman would trust a black man or vice versa."

"Times change, people change."

"I don't know, Harley. I just don't know."

"I know it's a lot to ask. Just let him stay, at least until we solve this case."

"And how long will that be, Harley?"

"I don't know."

"What about our friends and neighbors. What will they say when they find out we have a klansman living right under our roof?"

"Please, Roz. If you can't do it for me, then do it for Steve."

"Harley, I love you too much to say no to you."

"Does that mean he can stay?

"He can stay."

"Thanks, honey." He hugs her. "Come on. I'll introduce you."

They go into the living room. Stacy and Jamie are still on the sofa next to Jessup. "Stacy, take Jamie upstairs and get him ready for bed. I'll be up in a minute."

"Okay, mom. Good night, Mr. Jessup."

"Good night, Stacy."

They leave the room. "Roz, this is Harold Jessup."

"Mr. Jessup."

"Mrs. Jefferson."

"Mr. Jessup, I was very sorry to hear about your friend."

"Thank you, Mrs. Jefferson. That means a lot to me."

"Harley has told me a little about you."

"Mrs. Jefferson, I'm sure you're not used to having anyone like me in your home."

"You're right, Mr. Jessup, I'm not. My husband has told me of your situation and I've agreed to let you stay, at least until this case is solved."

"Thank you, Mrs. Jefferson. I promise I won't bother you or the kids. I'll stay in my room. You won't even know I'm here. I can even take my meals in my room."

"Mr. Jessup, this isn't a hotel. You'll eat with us. Is that understood?"

"Yes, Mrs. Jefferson."

"Another thing, Mr. Jessup. I think it's only fair that Stacy know who you are and why you're staying with us."

"I think so, too."

"Well, I'd better go check on the kids. Good night, Mr. Jessup."

"Good night, Mrs. Jefferson."

"Honey, I'll be up in a minute."

Roz leaves. "Wow! She's tough."

"Yeah. Wait until you see her on a bad day."

"If this is a good day, I would hate to see her bad days."

"Very wise. Hey, you want a beer?"

"Sure."

"Make yourself at home. I'll' be right back."

"Okay."

Harley goes toward the kitchen. Meanwhile, Roz and Stacy are seated on the bed in Stacy's beautiful peach bedroom. The nightstand contains a small lamp, a family portrait and an alarm clock. "Mom, who's that man downstairs?"

"He's the man who's been arrested for Steve's death."

"I didn't know someone had been arrested. He's not that klansman?"

"Yes, he is."

"What's he doing here? Shouldn't he be in jail?"

"He's out on bail."

"Yeah, but what's he doing here?"

"Your father brought him here. He's staying with us for a little while."

"Mom, how could daddy bring this man into our home," she says angrily, "and how could you let him?"

"Young lady, don't raise your voice to me."

"I'm sorry, mom."

"Your father and I talked it over and we agreed to let him stay."

"Why?"

"Apparently your father believes his life may be in danger."

"From who?"

"Your father feels that whoever killed Steve is now trying to harm Mr. Jessup."

"I thought he was the one who killed Steve."

"Well, so did your father. Then something happened which made him realize that someone else could be involved in Steve's death."

"What?"

"Mr. Jessup and another man were staying at a motel here in town. Tonight two men broke into their room. Mr. Jessup was beaten and his friend was killed."

"He told me he had gotten into a fight."

"Yeah."

"Why would someone do something like that?"

"Your father believes it was a warning."

"Of what?"

"Of danger."

"What kind of danger?"

"Well, one of the men threatened Mr. Jessup."

"Really."

"Yeah. He told him if he knew anything about Steve's death to keep his mouth shut or he'd be a dead man."

"So daddy really believes someone else killed Steve?"

"Yes, dear. Wouldn't you?"

"I suppose so, but what if Mr. Jessup lied."

"Why would he?"

"So no one would find out that he really killed Steve."

"Honey, I don't understand what you're implying?"

"Maybe his friend found out that he killed Steve and threatened to tell the police, so Mr. Jessup killed him so he wouldn't."

"Stacy, that sounds a little far-fetched to me."

"Maybe so, but it's possible."

"Honey, I think you want so much to believe he killed Steve, that you're just grasping at straws."

"Mom, please."

"Stacy, your father really believes this man is innocent and that someone else was responsible for Steve's death. Besides, don't you think your father deserves more credit than you're giving him. I think he would know if Mr. Jessup were lying. After all, he is a cop."

"I suppose you're right, mom, but why does he have to stay here? He's a klansman."

"He has to. Your father's protecting him."

"Couldn't he get a white cop to protect him?"

"He doesn't want to. He trusts your father and I believe your father trusts him, too."

"That's a switch."

"Please, honey, try to understand. Your father's only doing what he thinks is right."

"Just because it's right doesn't mean I have to like it."

Roz hugs Stacy. "I know, baby. I know."

Meanwhile, Harley returns with the beers. Jessup is standing in the hallway looking at the pictures on the wall. Harley hands him a beer. "Thanks." They go back into the living room and sit on the sofa. "Jefferson, you've got a real nice looking family."

"Thanks. What about you? Got any family?"

"One brother."

"Are you married?"

"I was, but she left me when I joined the Klan. I didn't think she would, but she did." He stares into space.

"I'm sorry to hear that."

"Yeah, so am I."

"I don't know what I'd do if Roz left me."

"Well, I don't think you'll have to worry about that."

"I hope not. So Jessup, what do you do for a living?"

"I'm an accountant."

"An accountant." He bursts out laughing.

"Yeah. What's wrong with that?"

"Nothing. I just can't picture you as an accountant."

"Why not?"

"Because I always pictured an accountant as being a skinny guy in a dark suit wearing thick glasses."

Jessup laughs. "Sorry to disappoint you."

"Well, we'd better get to bed. Come on. I'll show you where your room is."

"Okay."

11

The Jefferson family, along with Jessup, is seated at the breakfast table. The delicious aromas of fresh coffee, orange juice, toast, scrambled eggs and crisp bacon fill the room. Harley is seated at one end of the table, while Roz is seated at the other end. Stacy and Jamie are seated side by side. Jessup is seated across from them. "Mrs. Jefferson, this is a great breakfast."

"Thank you, Mr. Jessup."

"Stacy, are you okay? You're kind of quiet this morning."

"I'm fine, daddy." She glances at Jessup. The very sight of him sitting across from her leaves a sickening feeling in the pit of her stomach.

"How's school?"

"Daddy, it's okay."

"How are you coming along in math?"

"I'm doing better, mom."

"Stacy, if you need any help, I'd be glad to give you a hand. I'm an accountant and I'm real good with numbers."

"If I need any help, you'd be the last person I'd ask."

"Stacy, apologize to Mr. Jessup."

"No, daddy, I won't. We're all sitting here pretending everything's okay, but it's not. You don't belong here, Mr. Jessup, so why don't you just leave." She gets up from the table and runs upstairs.

"Stacy, come back here. I'm sorry about that, Mr. Jessup. She's still upset about Steve. He was her godfather and they were very close."

"It's okay, Mrs. Jefferson. I understand. She is right, you know. I don't belong here. I'll find another place to stay tonight. I don't want to cause any trouble."

"Perhaps it would be better." Phone rings. "I'll get it." She gets up to answer the phone. "Hello."

"I'd like to speak to Det. Jefferson."

"Just a moment. Honey, it's for you."

Harley comes to the phone. "Thanks, honey." She hands him the receiver. "Yeah."

"I want to talk to you about Steve Marks' murder. Meet me at the Magnolia Lounge in half an hour. Just ask for Weasel."

"Okay." He hangs up. "Jessup, we've got a lead. Come on. Let's go. Bye, honey." He kisses her on the cheek.

"You two be careful."

"We will."

They go outside and get into Harley's late model Ford Mustang. They back out of the driveway and are followed, from a distance, by Franklin in his light blue Ford Fairmont. Their car comes to a stop in front of the Magnolia Lounge. Franklin also stops his car at a distance, watches and waits. "Why are we stopping here?"

"That call I got was from a guy named Weasel. He wants to talk to me about Steve's murder."

"Do you think he knows anything?"

"I don't know." They get out of their car and go into the lounge. Franklin remains in his car. Once in the lounge, they go up to the bartender. He looks at Harley, then at Jessup, whom he recognizes from the altercation with Steve. He now glances back at Harley. "What can I do for you, Det. Jefferson?"

"I'm supposed to meet a guy named Weasel."

The bartender points to Weasel's table. "That's him over there."

"Thanks." They go over to Weasel's table. "Weasel, I'm Det. Jefferson and this is Harold Jessup."

Weasel eyes Jessup nervously. "I want to talk to you alone."

"It's okay, man. He's cool."

Weasel looks up at Jessup, then back at Harley. "Okay. He can stay." He motions for them to sit. They do.

"How well did you know Steve Marks?"

"Very well. I was his contact."

"Why didn't you come forward before?"

"I was afraid."

"Were you threatened?"

"No. Steve made sure no one knew my identity. I was safe."

"So why did you decide to come forward now?"

"Well, I figured Steve would want me to do the right thing."

"I'm sure he would."

"Besides, I heard you had a suspect."

"Yes, we do."

"I heard he was a klansman."

Harley glances at Jessup. "So what if he is?"

"I think he's innocent."

"I am innocent."

"You're the suspect."

"Yes."

"Oh, man, I'm sorry you had to be involved in this."

"So am I."

"I wish I had never given Steve that information. Maybe he would still be alive."

"What information?"

"The information about the drug deal."

"What drug deal?" asks Jessup.

"The one that went down in the park the night Steve was murdered."

"What!"

"Yeah. I met him here that night and I told him about the drug deal and the dirty cops."

Harley glances at Jessup. "Dirty cops!"

"Yeah."

"Which cops?" asks Jessup.

"I don't know."

"What do you know?"

"All I know is that some cops are selling drugs to some of the biggest dealers and pushers in town."

"Where would cops get drugs?" asks Jessup.

"Beats me."

"The evidence room. It's the only explanation that makes sense."

"Are you sure about that?" asks Jessup."

"Yes. That's where we keep the drugs we confiscate. Weasel, do you know any of the dealers or pushers involved?"

"I only know one dealer, but I don't know if he was involved."

"What's his name?"

"Tyrone Hudson."

"Yeah. That Jamaican. We've run him in a couple of times, but there was never enough evidence to make it stick."

"Did you say Jamaican?" asks Jessup.

"Yeah. Why?"

"You remember I told you that one of the guys who beat me had an accent."

"Yeah."

"I think it was Jamaican."

"So Tyrone is involved. Thanks, Weasel, you've been a great help."

"I'm glad I could help." As they get up from the table, Weasel spots Tyrone coming into the lounge. "Look! There's Tyrone." He points in Tyrone's direction.

Harley calls out to Tyrone from across the room. "Tyrone, we need to talk to you."

When Tyrone recognizes Harley, he runs out of the lounge. Harley and Jessup go after him. Tyrone is running down the sidewalk when Franklin, who is still in his car, spots him. He then notices Harley and Jessup running out of the lounge in Tyrone's direction. "Damn." He starts his car and follows along on the street. Suddenly Tyrone crosses the street. Franklin presses down on the accelerator and plows into Tyrone, who hits the front bumper, shattering the right headlight and bounces off the hood onto the street. Franklin keeps on going. Harley and Jessup run to Tyrone. Harley feels for a pulse. "How is he," asks Jessup.

"He's dead."

"Damn."

"Did you see the car?"

"No, I didn't. It all happened so fast."

By now a group of bystanders has gathered. "Did any of you see the car?" They all nod their heads. Suddenly Harley notices small light blue particles and tiny pieces of glass on Tyrone's clothing. "Take a look at these." He points them out to Jessup.

"What are they?"

"It looks like some paint chips and pieces of glass."

"Where did they come from?"

"Probably from the car that hit him."

"So it was a light blue car."

"Yeah. And Franklin has a light blue car."

"Do you think that was him?"

"I don't know. We still need more proof than this."

"So what do we do now?"

Harley hands Jessup his house key. "Here's my key. Go to the house and wait until I get there."

"Where are you going?"

"I'm going to check out the evidence room and then I'm going to the police parking lot to check out Franklin's car."

"Why can't I go with you?"

"Only authorized personnel allowed."

"Okay. Be careful."

"I will."

Harley arrives at the evidence room. There are rows of shelves each containing different types of confiscated evidence. At the entrance is a small desk and chair. On the desk is a tablet with a list of all evidence confiscated by the department. He picks up the tablet and goes down the list checking to make sure everything is in its place. "Five pounds of marijuana." He looks for it on the shelf. "Check." He goes on to the next item. "Ten pounds of cocaine." He looks in the place where it's supposed to be. "It's not here. Damn. I knew it."

Suddenly Sergeant Lou Rizzo, a stocky, bald italian, comes into the room. "Hey, Det. Jefferson."

"Lou, I didn't see you come in."

"Is there anything I can do for you?"

"No." He places the tablet back on the table. "I was just checking on some evidence."

"Sure."

"Lou, are you always at your desk?"

"Yes. The only time I leave is to go to the restroom. That's where I was when you got here."

"Do you leave your post for lunch?"

"I bring my lunch."

"Have you ever left your desk for more than fifteen minutes?"

"As a matter of fact one day last week."

"Why did you leave?"

"Capt. Rafferty wanted to see me in his office."

"Did you leave the desk alone?"

"No. He sent Franklin to cover for me."

"Thanks, Lou."

"I hope I'm not in any trouble."

"No, Lou. Everything's okay. If you see the captain, don't mention I was here."

"Okay, Det. Jefferson."

"Take care."

"You too."

Harley is in the basement parking lot. He spots Franklin's car. The first thing he notices is the busted headlight. He then notices something on the front bumper. He touches it. "Dried blood." He continues to examine the front area of the car. Suddenly he comes upon a spot on the hood where the paint is missing. Harley takes out a small, clear plastic bag and a pocket knife out of his coat pocket. He scrapes some of the dried blood into the bag. He then detaches a piece of glass from the headlight and lets it fall into the bag. Finally he scrapes a piece of loose paint from the hood and puts it in the bag. He seals the bag and places everything back in his pocket. He then leaves the area.

Harley enters the police crime lab. He is greeted by Carl, a forensic specialist with a string bean physique. Harley, what can I do for you?"

Harley takes out the plastic bag. "Do you have the evidence in the Tyrone Hudson case?"

"The only evidence I have are pieces of glass from a headlight and some light blue paint chips."

"In this bag I have a piece of glass and a paint chip. I want to know if these match the ones you took off of Tyrone's body."

"All right."

"I also have some dried blood in here."

"And you want to know if it matches Tyrone's blood type."

"That's right."

"How soon do you need this?"

"As soon as possible."

"Sure, Harley."

"I'll be home, so call me there."

"Okay, Harley."

Rafferty is standing at the front desk when Franklin comes in. "Did you follow them, Franklin?"

"Yeah and good thing I did."

"Why? Where did they go?"

"They went to the Magnolia Lounge to talk to Tyrone."

"How did they know about Tyrone?"

"I don't know."

"Damn. He's probably told them everything."

"He didn't get a chance to. I took care of him."

"Good, Franklin."

12

Jessup walks into the Jefferson home. He stops by the door of the living room and looks in. Stacy is on the floor dancing. She is wearing headphones which are connected to a small transistor radio that is fasten to her pants belt. Jamie is sitting on the floor playing with a yellow dump truck. Unnoticed, Jessup continues toward the stairs.

After listening to her music, Stacy sits on the sofa. She takes off the headphones and the radio and places them on the sofa next to her. Then she takes some money out of her right pants pocket and proceeds to count it. She counts the bills. "One, two, three, four, five, six, seven." She counts the coins. "Twenty-five, thirty, thirty-five, forty." She puts them on the sofa table. Phone rings. She stuffs the bills back in her pocket, leaves the coins on the table and gets up to answer the phone. "Hello." Jamie gets up and goes over to the table and starts playing with the coins.

"Hi, Stacy."

"Hi, mom. I thought you'd be home by now."

"So did I, honey, but it's so crowded here at the supermarket. Could you put the roast in the oven and set the timer? I'll be home directly."

"Sure, mom."

"Thanks, honey. See you later."

"Okay." She hangs up the phone. When she turns around, she finds Jamie on the floor unconscious. She runs to him. "Jamie, are you okay?" He isn't breathing. Stacy then notices a couple of coins on the floor near him. She places both hands on her mouth. "Oh, my God." She gets up and runs toward the door screaming hysterically. "Help me. Please, somebody, help me."

She is at the door when Jessup comes running down the stairs. He grabs her by the shoulders. "What happened?"

She is crying so much she can barely speak. "It's... It's Jamie."

Jessup runs into the living room and kneels by Jamie. "He isn't breathing. What happened?" Before she can answer, he sees the coins and figures it out. "Oh, God. Stacy, did Jamie swallow one of these coins?"

"Yes."

"Okay. Calm down. Go over to the phone and dial 911. Hurry."

"Okay."

While she calls 911, Jessup tilts back Jamie's head, pinches his nostrils and begins mouth to mouth resuscitation. Every now and then he checks Jamie's breathing. "Breathe, Jamie, breathe." When there's no response from Jamie, Jessup tries another method. With the fingers of both hands pointing toward Jamie's head, Jessup places the heel of his right hand on Jamie's abdomen and places his left hand on top of the right. He presses down on Jamie's abdomen with four quick thrusts. Then he opens Jamie's mouth with his left hand, and with the index finger of his right hand formed in the shape of a hook, he reaches deeply into Jamie's throat at the base of the tongue. "I feel something." He dislodges the coin and pulls it out. "Got it."

Jamie coughs. Stacy is at his side. "Jamie, I'm so glad you're okay." There is a knock at the door. "I'll get it. It's probably the paramedics."

She goes to the door, opens it and lets them in. One is a man and the other is a woman. Both are dressed in white and the woman is carrying a first aid kit. "Where's the choking victim?" asks the woman.

"Right this way."

They follow Stacy into the living room. "How is he?" asks the man.

"Well, I think he's okay," says Jessup. "I managed to get the coin out."

"Well, young lady," says the woman, "looks like you didn't need us after all."

Suddenly Harley and Roz burst into the house and run into the living room. They see the paramedics tending to Jamie. They run to him. "Jamie," says Harley.

"Oh, my baby."

"Stacy, what happened?" asks Harley.

Before she can utter a single word, Jessup answers. "I'm afraid it was all my fault."

Stacy is blown away by his statement.

"I left some coins on the coffee table and Jamie accidentally swallowed one of them."

Roz puts both hands over her mouth in fear. "Oh, no. Is my baby going to be okay?"

"He's going to be just fine, ma'am," says the man.

"Thank God."

"I really feel bad about everything. It was very careless of me."

"Yes, it was very careless," says Roz. "Jamie could've died."

"I know that, Mrs. Jefferson, and I want you to know how...."

Stacy realizes she can't let Jessup lie for her anymore. "Stop"

Her parents are bewildered by Stacy's sudden outburst. "What's wrong, honey?" asks Roz.

Stacy's eyes fill with tears. "Mr. Jessup didn't leave the coins on the table. I did."

"Oh, Stacy," says Roz.

"I didn't mean to. I just got up to answer the phone and I forgot them on the table. I'm so sorry."

"We know you're sorry, Stacy," says Roz, "but that's not the point. The point is that you're supposed to be taking care of your little brother. He's too young to understand right from wrong, so it's your job to watch over him and make sure things like this don't happen."

"I know, mom. I promise it won't happen again."

"I hope not, honey."

"Thank you both so much," says Harley to the paramedics.

"Don't thank us," says the woman. "Thank him." She points to Jessup. "He saved your son's life. We didn't do anything."

"Yeah," says the man. "He had already removed the coin from Jamie's throat when we arrived." The paramedics close up their kit. "Good day." They leave.

The Jefferson family now see Jessup in a whole new light. "Mr. Jessup," says Roz, "I don't know how I'll ever be able to thank you for saving my baby's life."

"You don't have to, Mrs. Jefferson. The look on your face is thanks enough." Roz smiles.

"Jessup, I'll never forget what you did for Jamie. Thanks."

"Thank you so much, Mr. Jessup. I just hope you can forgive me for the way I acted at breakfast this morning."

"Stacy, I already have."

She smiles.

"Mr. Jessup," says Roz, "if you'd like to stay with us a little while longer, we'd be glad to have you."

"Yes, we would," says Stacy.

"Okay, I'll stay."

"Great."

"Well, I'd better check on dinner. Stacy, take Jamie upstairs and get him cleaned up for dinner."

"Okay, mom."

Roz, Stacy and Jamie all exit the room.

"So what did you find out about Franklin?"

"A lot. I checked the evidence room. There's some cocaine missing and I know for a fact that Franklin took it."

"Did you check his car?"

"Yeah."

"Is it the same car that ran down Tyrone?"

"I'm almost positive it is. The right headlight was busted. There was a spot on the hood where there wasn't any paint and I found dried blood on the front bumper. I took a piece of glass, a paint chip and some dried blood to the lab to have it analyzed. I'm awaiting the results." Knock at the door. "I'll get it." He leaves the room to answer the door. When he opens the door, he comes face to face with Warren Brooks. "Mr. Brooks."

"Det. Jefferson, I need to speak to you."

"Sure. Come in."

Brooks comes in. "Thanks."

Harley shuts the door. "Let's go into the living room." Brooks follows Harley into the living room. When he walks in and spots Jessup, a displeasing look comes over his face. "You remember Mr. Jessup."

"Of course. Mr. Jessup."

"Mr. Brooks."

Brooks glances around the room. "Det. Jefferson, you've got a real nice home."

"Thank you, Mr. Brooks, but I'm sure you didn't come here just to talk about my home."

"You're right."

"I thought we said everything that needed saying."

"I thought so, too, but then I heard this rumor, so I decided to come over and check it out."

"What rumor?"

Brooks looks Jessup squarely in the eyes. "I heard that Mr. Jessup was staying with you. Is that true?"

"Not that it's any of your business, but yes, he is staying with us."

"I don't think I've ever heard of anything so bizarre in all my life."

"Mr. Jessup is under my protection."

"Protection from who?"

"I think I can answer that for you," responds Jessup.

"Please do."

"Last night two men broke into my motel room. I was beaten and my roommate was killed. One of the men told me that if I knew anything about Steve Marks' murder to keep my mouth shut or I'd be a dead man."

"Why don't you tell us how it really happened?"

"Just what are you trying to say?"

"Maybe you killed your friend, because he found out you killed Steve Marks and he threatened to go to the police."

"I don't care what you think. I didn't kill him."

"He's telling the truth."

"Okay, maybe he is, but how can you trust this klansman with your family?"

"I'll tell you how. A couple of minutes before my wife and I came home, our four year old son swallowed a coin and if it hadn't been for this klansman, my son would have choked to death."

"I didn't know that."

"Of course you didn't. You're too busy condemning him. Whatever happened to innocent until proven guilty? If he's guilty of anything, it's racism, not murder."

"You've got a point there, Detective. Mr. Jessup, I'm afraid I may have been wrong about you after all. Please accept my apology."

"Apology accepted."

"I'm afraid I let my personal views cloud my judgement."

"I think we've all been guilty of that at one time or another," says Jessup.

"Yes, we have," agrees Harley.

"Well, good evening, gentlemen."

"Good evening."

Brooks leaves. "Thanks for standing up for me. It meant a lot to me."

"It's the least I can do for the man who saved my son's life." Phone rings. "That's probably the lab." He answers the phone. "Hello."

"Harley, it's Carl."

"Yeah, Carl. What have you got?"

"Well, the piece of glass and the paint chip you gave me matches the ones found on Tyrone's clothing."

"Good. What about the dried blood?"

"It's a perfect match."

"Thanks, Carl."

"Anytime, Harley."

Harley hangs up the phone. "The piece of glass and the paint chip I got off of Franklin's car matches the ones found on Tyrone's clothing. Also, the dried blood from his car matches Tyrone's blood type."

"Great. We've got him now. So what are we going to do?"

"We're going to pay him a visit."

"You think he'll talk."

"He has no choice. We have proof."

13

Harley and Jessup arrive at Franklin's home. They get out of the car. "You go around back and make sure he doesn't try to get away."

"Okay." Jessup goes around to the back of the house, while Harley goes up to the front door and rings the doorbell.

Franklin is standing at the kitchen sink drinking a glass of water. "Who is it?"

"Det. Jefferson."

Franklin senses that something is wrong. "I'll be right there." But instead of going to the front door, he heads to the back door. When he opens the door, he unexpectedly comes face to face with Jessup. Meanwhile at the front door, Harley tries the doorknob. It turns. He goes in. Franklin makes his way back to the front with a little help from Jessup.

"He tried to make a run for it," announces Jessup.

"No. I was just going to put out the trash."

Jessup smiles and shakes his head.

"Somehow, I don't believe you," says Harley.

"I don't care what you believe."

Meanwhile outside, Rafferty has just arrived. He spots Harley's car in the yard. "I wonder what Harley's doing here." He goes around to the back. He slowly turns the knob on the back door and goes in. He creeps into the room adjacent to where the others are talking and listens attentively to their conversation.

Meanwhile, Harley and Jessup are questioning Franklin.

"Franklin, why don't you just tell the truth."

"The truth about what?"

"About everything."

"I don't know what you're talking about."

"Sure you do," says Jessup. "You see I saw you the night you came to my motel room. The night I was beaten and Jake was killed."

"I was never in your motel room."

"Yes, you were. You took the stocking off your face before walking out the door. I bet you didn't think I saw you, but I did."

"We now know the guy with you was Tyrone Hudson," says Harley.

"What would I be doing with a known drug dealer?"

"You were partners in crime," answers Jessup.

"You stole drugs from the evidence room and you sold them to Tyrone. Steve found out about it and that's why he was killed. Then when we tried to talk to Tyrone, you ran him down."

"You can't prove that."

"Oh, but I can. I took a look at your car. Your right headlight was busted. The paint on the hood was chipped and there was dried blood on the front bumper. I took a piece of glass from the headlight, a paint chip from the hood and the dried blood and I brought it to the lab. I just received the results. The glass and paint matched the glass and paint found on Tyrone's clothing and the dried blood matched Tyrone's blood type."

"You'd better start talking," says Jessup.

"How many cops are involved?"

"One more besides me."

"Who is he?"

"Capt. Rafferty."

"Capt. Rafferty! I can't believe this."

"Well, you can believe it. It was all his idea. He was the mastermind behind the whole operation. I would steal the drugs from the evidence room and we would sell them to the dealers and pushers."

"What happened the night of Steve's murder?"

"We met with Tyrone in the park and we cut a deal, but Steve was there, also. He had photographed the whole transaction. We had to kill him."

"Who killed Steve?"

"Capt. Rafferty."

"This is unbelievable. I've known Capt. Rafferty all my life and I even looked up to him. He was my role model. I guess I never really knew him."

"I sometimes wonder if it's possible for one person to ever really know another person."

"I hope so, because if it weren't, this world would be in much worse shape than it already is."

Both men come back to reality.

"We know you killed Tyrone, but who killed Jake?"

"That was an accident. I didn't mean to kill him, I swear. I didn't know he was dead until I returned to your motel room to investigate."

Jessup lunges at Franklin grabbing him by the neck. "You bastard!"

Harley tries to pull Jessup away from Franklin. "Let him go. He's not worth it."

Jessup lets go of Franklin.

"Franklin, will you swear to all this in court?"

"Yes."

"Let's go. You have the right…"

Suddenly Rafferty comes into the room. He is holding a .38 caliber revolver with a silencer attached to it. "Hold, it right there."

Franklin is relieved to see him. "Captain, thank God you're here."

"Franklin, you told them everything."

"No, captain. They already knew."

Rafferty shoots Franklin. He falls to the floor, his bloody hands clutching his abdomen.

"You won't get away with this," says Harley.

"You know I underestimated you two." He motions for them to move. "Come on. Let's go."

"Where are we going?" asks Jessup.

"That's for me to know and you to find out." They go out the door toward Rafferty's car. They are about to get in the car when Rafferty hands Harley the keys. "Get in. Harley, you drive. Jessup, you get in the back."

Harley gets in the driver's seat, while Jessup sits in the back seat behind Harley. Rafferty sits next to Jessup. They leave Franklin's house and pass through the downtown area. "Where do you want me to turn?"

"Just drive, Harley. I'll let you know when it's time to turn."

"Why, captain? You were a good cop once. What happened?"

"I was a good cop once, but that was a long time ago. Then I started seeing all my friends with good jobs making lots of money, more money than I could ever dream of making. All I had was a lousy cop's salary. Do you know how hard it is to raise a family on that?"

"Yes, I do."

"It's damn near impossible. The worst thing was seeing the look on my kids' faces when I told them I couldn't afford to buy them new things like their friends had."

Harley and Jessup listen to Rafferty with a certain degree of compassion.

"I'm sure they understood," says Harley.

"Understood. How in the hell do you expect a kid to understand something like that? Even if they did, that's not the point. The point is that I was the breadwinner and I should have been able to provide for all their needs. So from that moment on, I decided I would find a way to make sure my family would never have to want for anything."

"If you weren't making enough money, why didn't you just quit and get another job, instead of doing what you did."

"Quit and do what, Harley? Being a cop was all I knew. I did what I had to. I don't expect you or anyone else to understand." For a moment there is silence. "Turn left at the next light."

Harley turns left. "This road leads out of town." Rafferty doesn't answer.

"What are you going to do with us?" asks Jessup.

"You're bright enough. Figure it out."

"Hasn't there been enough killing?"

"Harley, just shut up and drive." They are now driving through a wooded area. Just a few feet ahead is an orange barricade with two

90

flashing yellow lights. The writing on the barricade says: DANGER, BRIDGE OUT, DO NOT ENTER. A white arrow with the word DETOUR written on it points to the right. Harley looks up at Jessup in the rear view mirror. With Jessup following his lead, Harley's eyes leave the rear view mirror and travel to the barricade, then back to the rear view mirror. They have communicated without uttering a single word. Suddenly Harley presses down on the accelerator. "Slow down, Harley. Don't you see that barricade up ahead?" But Harley doesn't let up on the accelerator. When Rafferty sees that Harley won't slow down, he points the gun at his head. "Slow down, Harley or I'll blow your head off." Jessup grabs Rafferty and they begin to struggle. Jessup delivers a right punch to the left side of Rafferty's jaw. Rafferty falls back into the seat. The gun falls out of his hand onto the floor. Meanwhile, they are approaching the barricade.

"Jump, Jessup," hollers Harley. Harley and Jessup both jump out of the car. As the car nears the barricade, Rafferty raises his arms in front of his face and screams. The car goes through the barricade, plunges into the river and sinks.

14

A cab with the words Yellow Cab written on both doors stops in front of the Jefferson home. Jessup gets out, walks up to the front door and knocks. Stacy opens the door. "Hi, Mr. Jessup."

"Hi, Stacy."

"Come in."

"Thank you, Stacy."

He goes in. As she is shutting the door, she notices the cab parked outside. "Come on. Everyone's in the living room." He follows her into the living room. "Hey, everybody, look who's here," she says gleefully. Harley and Roz are seated on the sofa and Jamie is seated between them.

"Mr. Jessup, come in and have a seat," says Roz.

"Thank you, Mrs. Jefferson." He sits on the loveseat next to Stacy.

"Jessup, where have you been? I haven't seen you since you went back to your motel room."

"Well, I had to take care of some unfinished business."

"I've been trying to reach you to let you know that the DA formally dropped the murder charge against you."

"Yeah. I read about it and also about Franklin's confession in the paper this morning."

"I'm just relieved that everything is finally over," says Harley.

"So am I," says Jessup.

"Wasn't it nice that the <u>Gazette</u> gave Steve credit for breaking the story?"

"Yes, it was," says Jessup.

"He deserved it," says Harley.

"He sure did," agrees Roz.

"Mr. Jessup, you'll never guess what happened," says Stacy.

"What?"

"Daddy made captain," Stacy announces proudly.

"Congratulations, Jefferson. You must be very happy."

"Not exactly. More like bittersweet."

"Well, I can understand that."

"Would you like to stay for lunch, Mr. Jessup?"

"I'm afraid I can't, Mrs. Jefferson."

"Is that your cab parked outside?" asks Stacy.

"Yes, it is."

"Are you leaving?"

"Yes, I am, Stacy."

"Jessup, I thought you'd be staying for the march. Isn't it today?"

"Yes, it is, but I won't be staying for it."

The family glances curiously at each other.

"I don't understand," says Harley. "Isn't that why you came to Clarion?"

"Yes, in the beginning it was, but things have changed. I've changed. That's why I've decided to leave the Klan."

Never in their wildest dreams could the Jefferson family have ever imagined such a statement.

"Really, Mr. Jessup?" asks a pleasantly surprised Stacy.

His smile reassures her. "Really, Stacy."

"That's great, Mr. Jessup."

"Yeah. What made you decide to leave, Jessup?"

"You did, Jefferson."

"Me. How?"

"When I was growing up, my parents told me that blacks were inferior to whites. They said that blacks were lazy and always up to no good and that I should never trust them. Then I met you and your family. You weren't anything like my parents had described. Instead, I found a hard working family man, trustworthy and reliable. A man who brought me into his home when I needed help, even though he didn't have to. A man who put his reputation and his life on the line for me. No one has ever done that for me. No one."

"I would do it again."

"Well, you wouldn't be the kind of man you are if you didn't." He glances at the family with admiration. "Jefferson, you've got a beautiful family. I envy you, but at the same time, I've come to respect you."

"Thank you. The feeling is mutual."

"With your friend dead and you no longer in the Klan," says Roz, "I have to wonder if they're still coming."

"Oh, they'll come," says Jessup. "They want an audience."

"Well, they've come to the wrong place," says Stacy.

Jessup is puzzled by her remark. "What do you mean by that, Stacy?"

"There won't be an audience today."

"You haven't heard the news?" asks Roz.

"What news?"

"Brooks called me early this morning."

"What did he want?"

"He said the town council had an emergency meeting last night to discuss the march. They voted unanimously to close all businesses in town today."

"We can't stop them from marching," says Roz, "but we can stop them from shopping in our stores, eating in our restaurants, buying our gas…"

"And even from using our public restrooms," says Stacy.

Everyone laughs.

"It all sounds so drastic," says Jessup. "Saturday is usually a pretty busy day and with the economy the way it is, you're taking a pretty big risk. Do you think it's worth it? "

"Yeah, it's worth it, even if we have to lose some money, because we want this to be the Klan's first and last visit to Clarion."

"I'm sure it will be."

"Also," adds Stacy, "every business will have an orange ribbon on its front door."

"Why orange?"

"Because orange is the international color for peace and brotherhood."

"I didn't know that."

"Don't feel bad, Jessup. I didn't know that either."

"Well," says Stacy, "you learn something new every day."

"You sure do, Stacy."

"So where are you headed now, Mr. Jessup?"

"I'm on my way to see my ex-wife. I called her last night and told her that I'd left the Klan. I also told her that I was finally putting my life back in perspective and that I wanted another chance. She said we could talk."

"That's great, Mr. Jessup. I hope everything works out for you."

"Thank you, Mrs. Jefferson. Well, I'd better get going."

They get up and walk Jessup to the door.

"Take care, Mr. Jessup."

"You too, Mrs. Jefferson." He bends down to say goodbye to Jamie. "Goodbye, Jamie." He places his right hand on Jamie's curly head of hair and musses it a little. Jamie coyly buries his face on his mother's left leg. Roz smiles. "He's so shy."

"Goodbye, Stacy."

The young girl places her arms around his waist and hugs him. "Goodbye, Mr. Jesssup. I'm going to miss you."

"So will I, Stacy."

Finally, both men are facing each other.

"You're one helluva man, Harley Jefferson."

"So are you, Harold Jessup."

"I'm never going to forget you."

"Nor I you."

Jessup extends his hand to Harley. "Take care, Harley."

Harley shakes his hand firmly. "You too, Harold."

They follow Jessup outside. He walks to his awaiting cab and gets in. They wave as the cab drives away.

15

The cab comes to a stop at an intersection. A police officer is blocking traffic. The black, broad shouldered cab driver, wearing a small, gray knit hat, is very upset. He hits the steering wheel with both hands. "Damn! I can't believe I forgot about that march. Hey, mister, you're not in too much of a hurry?"

"No."

The downtown area resembles a ghost town. The streets and sidewalks are vacant. An orange ribbon hangs on every closed door of every business.

The klansmen are coming down the street heading west. They are surrounded by city police officers wearing riot gear. The klansmen are dressed in their white hooded robes. The klan emblem is on the left front of their robes. It is a white cross enclosed in a red circle. The center of the cross is formed in the shape of a diamond with a red dot in the center of the diamond. Some of the klansmen hold Confederate flags in their left hands, while others hold flags bearing the Klan emblem. With palms down, their right hands are extended out above their heads in the Hail Hitler salute. As they march, they chant: "White power. White power." They now pass in front of the cab.

"Who'd ever thought the Klan would be marching in downtown Clarion," says the cab driver. "It just shows you how much things haven't really changed."

"Oh, but they have, my friend," replies Jessup. "They have."

The cab driver looks up at Jessup in the rear view mirror and flashes him a puzzled 1ook.

After all the klansmen have passed, the cab turns east. Jessup never looks back. Pretty soon the klansmen fade from view.

About the Author

My Brother's Keeper is Mary Bertha Attole's first novel. She credits her family and her devout Catholic faith as the main reasons for writing this book. Which is why the dedication in her book reads: To my family and my Catholic faith. Miss Attole hopes that people who read this book will realize that racism is not only ethically wrong, but also morally wrong. She has also written the screenplay version of this book. In addition to writing, Miss Attole loves reading, keeping up with current events, cooking, telling jokes, taking care of her pets, and doing weekly volunteer work at her local church, St. Mathilda Catholic Church, where she is a proud member. Miss Attole describes herself as "just a simple country girl and proud of it." She was born and raised in the Creole community of Mallet in southwestern Louisiana. Her devout Catholic parents spoke only French, so Miss Attole was taught English by her school teachers. She now lives in Eunice, La. with her mother Elia Guillory Attole, her brother Anthony Attole, and her sister Mary Ann Attole. Her father Antoine Attole is deceased.